Frozen

by Lucy Shepard
illustrated by Angela Adams

Core Decodable 67

Bothell, WA • Chicago, IL • Columbus, OH • New York, NY

MHEonline.com

Copyright © 2015 McGraw-Hill Education

All rights reserved. No part of this publication may be reproduced or distributed in any form or by any means, or stored in a database or retrieval system, without the prior written consent of McGraw-Hill Education, including, but not limited to, network storage or transmission, or broadcast for distance learning.

Send all inquiries to:
McGraw-Hill Education
8787 Orion Place
Columbus, OH 43240

ISBN: 978-0-02-144317-8
MHID: 0-02-144317-3

Printed in the United States of America.

2 3 4 5 6 7 8 9 DOC 20 19 18 17 16 15

Chad felt sad and alone.

He wished winter was over.

Did Mom go out?
Did Mom have a hose?

Chad looked in his yard.
A big spot was open.

Mom filled the open spot.
It froze hard. It froze so fast!

The entire yard had frozen.
Mom had made an ice rink!

Mom and Chad skated in the yard.
"I hope winter lasts!" said Chad.